We need SAI Forever... at 6, 16 and 60!

Saurabh Khanna

STERLING

STERLING PAPERBACKS
An imprint of
Sterling Publishers (P) Ltd.
Regd. Office: A1/256 Safdarjung Enclave,
New Delhi-110029. CIN: U22110DL1964PTC211907
Tel: 26387070, 26386209; Fax: 91-11-26383788
E-mail: mail@sterlingpublishers.com
www.sterlingpublishers.com

We need SAI Forever... at 6, 16 and 60!

ISBN 978 93 86245 15 1

Printed in India

Printed and Published by Sterling Publishers Pvt. Ltd.,
Plot No. 13, Ecotech-III, Greater Noida - 201306,
Uttar Pradesh, India

Dedication

I would like to dedicate this book as an offering to the lotus feet of Shirdi Sai as nothing belongs to me. It is a gift for my Sai on His centenary celebrations of taking Mahasamadhi in 1918. I would like to also offer my ego at the divine feet of Sai as I am just a mere instrument in His hands to pen down this book.

Acknowledgement

First of all, I would like to thank, from the deepest core of my heart, Samarth Sadguru Shirdi Sai Himself, Who entered my heart and inspired me to pen down the words in the form of this book for the benefit of all. At the same time, I would like to thank all the devotees of Sai, who kept interacting with me about their personal experiences and strengthened my conviction that this book was certainly needed. I would fall short in my duty if I do not thank my family, relatives, friends, and all the others who supported me in this endeavour. Last but not the least, would like to thank all my readers.

Contents

Chapter 1

Why This Book?

On a Thursday, Sai inspired me to write this book, and today, on the auspicious occasion of Basant Panchami, holding my heart and hand, He wants me to put pen to paper, with the blessings of the Goddess of Wisdom, Saraswati. Sai and Saraswati are not different. They are forms of the same Supreme Power.

Why has Sai inspired me to write a book on Him when there is innumerable literature on Him already available? This is a very important question that needs to be answered. In today's world, when everyone is trying to find logic in everything, if this question remains unanswered, it will definitely create restlessness.

Well, my dear readers, this book is written keeping the youth in mind. This, in no way, means that the book is not meant for others.

I am 42 years old, but my connection with Sai was first made when I was a young lad of 21. Baba has inspired me to write this book, more than two decades after my first encounter with Him. I feel happy to take this as an opportunity to let the world know that in almost all phases of my life, I have experienced His invaluable help or *kripa* (mercy or grace).

My young friends must realize why they need Sai at such a young and tender age. The reasons are many. We are all entangled in innumerable desires, which range from career to relationships and much more. There is not a single phase in life where we are not faced with a crisis. And who can rescue us in such situations? Only our Sai, no one else.

Sai says that whenever we are in trouble, we should just remember Him at that moment and He will certainly reveal and present Himself to us.

When I came into contact with Sai, I was only 21. It was the turning point of my life, indeed. So it is natural for me to share that experience with my readers. It was an event that proved to be my biggest and everlasting blessing. Such is the *leela* (the ways) of my Sai.

The *leelas* of Sai are beyond comprehension of a normal human mind. The more you try to understand them, the more confused you become. This is mainly because we try to use our limited mind and limited resources to understand the infinite through our finite senses. Surrendering ourselves at the lotus feet of Sai, slowly and steadily, with conviction, is the ideal thing to do.

Everyone enjoys freedom. But in spirituality, real freedom is achieved by surrendering one's freedom to the Sadguru (the real spiritual master). Then one is really free, and light as a feather.

It is also important to use the word *Sadguru* very carefully. Let us first understand what the word *Guru* means. Guru is made up of two Sanskrit words or syllables, *Gu* and *Ru*. *Gu* signifies ignorance and *Ru* signifies the one who counteracts or dispels ignorance. Thus, *Guru* is the one who removes all ignorance.

Guru also refers to the one who gives us enlightenment. Our basic nature is already pure and wise. It is only because of the karmic actions in different lives that we become ignorant of our true self or nature. Sadguru is the one who makes us realize the Sat—the eternal truth. Sai is a *Samarth* Sadguru. *Samarth* means capable of handing out knowledge in a way that we are able to understand it.

To give an analogy, we are like the ever-shining diamond whose lustre is lost over many births because of the impurities on it. The Sadguru is responsible for removing these impurities and bringing back our own shine and original nature. This is the real journey of life.

My Sai has become an indispensable part of me now. My passion for my Sadguru has increased with time and I consider myself extremely blessed and lucky to have been able to establish a strong relationship with

Him. Sai has changed His position and role according to my needs. I only realized that Guru was God through a series of incidents, which are not only coincidental and supernatural, but blessed through Sai.

Think of Him always. He will take care of you.

Chapter 2

Life's Nuances

It all started in October 1994, when I was in the seventh semester of the engineering course I was doing in Maharashtra, India. I started getting peculiar thoughts and lost peace of mind, reaching a severe state of psychotic depression. Some people suggested the cause as black magic, perhaps by a jealous rival who wanted my attention to be diverted from studies. After all, I had stood first in my college for six consecutive semesters. I was a popular student, and very close to my professors.

I became miserable and sleep-deprived, having spent 21 nights without sleep. I thought I had gone mad and wanted to quit the college altogether. I tried every remedy, without success. It was with a lot of fear and nervousness that I sat for my examinations for the seventh semester. To my complete surprise, when the results were declared, I had stood first once again, with a margin of five marks over the next student.

I used to visit Shirdi every semester. In these visits, I looked at Sai as a God. When my seventh semester results were declared, I saw Sai smiling at me from His photo, which I had brought from Shirdi, and tears started streaming from my eyes. My faith was re-confirmed. This was the first time I felt there was much more to Sai than just a God. He was, in fact, a Sadguru too. God did exist. When my mother heard about the results, she exclaimed joyfully, "God is great!" I am grateful for the continuous support of my parents, my family, and friends.

From here commenced my journey towards my Sadguru's divine feet, for He always says, "Surrender, and I will take care. Why do you fear when I am here?"

The most famous and reliable literature from the time when Sai was physically present in this mortal world is the *Sai Satcharitra*. Sai inspired the book to be written and documented for the betterment of humankind. Apart from other important issues, it describes the effects of karma and how Sai was taking their impact upon Himself for the welfare of His devotees.

The Bhagavad Gita, narrated by Lord Krishna for the benefit of His devotee Arjuna, on the battlefield of Kurukshetra, also defines karma (actions) as *Sanchit, Prarabdh* and *Karmana* and how they are beautifully arranged.

Sanchit refers to the accumulated karmas whose reactions are yet to fructify; these are the karmas kept in reserve for future births. They will not fructify in this birth. *Prarabdh* for future births is a part of the *Sanchit* karmas.

Prarabdh are the karmas whose reactions are decided and put in place at the time of our birth, in the present life. These are the karmas we are born with. We have to face their consequences as a part of our earlier karmas. When, at times, we wonder why certain things are happening in our life despite not doing anything to cause them, they are all because of *Prarabdh*. *Prarabdh* can be both positive and negative. Thus, it is plainly a partial effect on the present life, of what we did in earlier births. It is actually what is termed as *destiny*.

Karmana are the karmas we perform with our so-called free will in this birth and whose reactions will certainly come to us in this life, or can be transformed later into *Sanchit* or *Prarabdh* for future times. In other words, *Karmana* may turn into results in this life or may be carried forward as *Prarabdh* or *Sanchit* for future lives. While *Sanchit* can be nullified, how *Prarabdh's* intensity can be lessened and *Karmana* performed as karma yoga can be nullified, are all explained through spiritual texts.

Sai teaches us that through devotion, we can nullify *Sanchit* karmas as they haven't fructified and were kept in reserve. However, we have to necessarily undergo

Prarabdh. Though Sai can reduce its effects, He can't make it zero. We should perform *Karmana* with Sai as the centre of our thoughts and then they will not be carried forward as *Sanchit* and *Prarabdh*. In this case, Sai becomes the doer and not us. Thus, offering all the karmas to Sai is the key, but this does not mean that we are troubling Sai. He considers this His very purpose. Till all karmas don't nullify, *moksha* or salvation is impossible, which is the aim of human life and can only be attained in the human form.

However, the mysteries involved in all these processes can only be revealed through Sadguru's grace. Once *Sanchit, Prarabdh* and *Karmana* become zero, which means their reactions are nullified, the soul becomes ready to attain moksha or salvation through Sadguru's *kripa*. In fact, this process, termed as self-realization, is the very reason for the purpose of human birth.

The Bhagavad Gita also talks about this. Emotions are natural. At the battlefield of Kurukshetra, Arjuna, who had actually been waiting to fight against his cousins, the Kauravas, suddenly lost all composure. When the time came to fight, he wanted to escape from his karma. He was disturbed. Krishna encouraged him to understand all his doubts. Krishna was ready to explain everything. According to him, if one goes to the Sadguru with the intention to learn, all the *agyan* (lack of knowledge) will be removed. Krishna took it upon himself to guide Arjuna just when he had lost all hope. Arjuna, on the other hand, surrendered himself completely to Lord Krishna and emerged victorious. Krishna acted as the Supreme Guide.

The more we try to find answers to why certain things are happening in our lives, the more confused we get. The answers are never available with clarity. They are all attributed to the eternal philosophy of karma, which is very complicated. We all know that life is full of nuances and finer meanings, but nobody knows their exact nature. So, what do we do?

God's reasons and *leelas* are beyond the comprehension of our limited intellect. An individual suffers because of her or his own karmas. The sufferings come in the form of *Tan* (body), *Mann* (mind) and *Dhan* (wealth).

We are actually souls who are a part of the Super Soul (*Par-Atma*).The tiny wave looks at the vast ocean and cries on realizing its limitations, but is it really any different from the ocean? Similarly, our composition is the same as that of the Super Soul, only a bit limited.

We will continue to suffer as long we think that we are merely the body. When I say, "I am Saurabh", who is the "I" and who is "Saurabh"? It is important to know the real "I".

All *sadhana* (efforts to achieve self-realization) is focussed on removing this *avidya* (ignorance), which causes sorrow. As long as the body is there, we will feel its agony—hunger, thirst, disease, and so on. These are unavoidable and this is the hard truth. If the body and mind do not exist, how can we experience the reactions of our actions or karmas?

As long as *avidya* remains, we suffer. Once it vanishes, the sufferings of the body stop bothering us. The true saints of the ancient times lived in this state all the time—Kabir, Namdev, Tukaram, Tulsidas, Surdas, Ramana Maharishi, Vivekanand, and so many others.

When the body and mind are suffering, it is impossible for the individual to remain unaffected. All *sadhana*—our efforts to achieve self-realization—is geared towards removing the illusion which makes us feel that we are only the body, whereas the body is just a covering superimposed on our pure state.

Our unlimited desires—*vasanas*—are hard to dissolve, but not trying to remove them will only strengthen them. Is it possible to remove them? Actually, we have to reach a state of desirelessness, which means change the course of our desires and focus on the desire of being constantly at the lotus feet of the Sadguru.

The Vedas say *"Chare Vedic, Chare Vedic"*—march on, march on. We have to keep moving forward towards our goal. The moment we tell ourselves that it is too hard to achieve that pure state, we end up stuck in the cavern of this world. However, the more we try, the more grace pours in to help us along the way.

Rumi, a very famous Sufi saint said, "What you seek is seeking you."

Sai said, "Take one step and I take umpteen steps towards you."

Naam (Name of the Lord) is the boat you sit on to cross the ocean of *samsara* (the physical world). We should not consider leaving this world before the time comes. Sai, in the *Satcharitra,* clearly spoke against suicides, saying it is better to suffer and ensure that the reactions to your karmas are nullified in this birth itself rather than carry them forward to the next birth. Till the time we do not bear the fruits of our karmas, we have no escape. This is in the same context of *Sanchit, Prarabdh,* and *Karmana* and their reactions, as described earlier. If you don't succeed in nullifying the reactions to your karmas, you will have to carry them for the next birth. In today's world, we witness so many suicides among all age-groups, especially the youth. If they seek Sai's help, I am sure their lives will improve manifold. It's the simple things that are the most powerful. Try the *naam smaran*. Even Buddhism follows the practice of chanting.

Kaliyug keval naam adhara,
Sumir sumir nar utrahi para,
Sumir sumir nar pavhi para.

In the present era of Kaliyug, taking the Lord's name is the most efficient and easiest way to attain salvation. Each Yuga has its own practical path.

While reading all this philosophy, we should not forget that truth is simple. Often, we are reading and not implementing; hearing and not listening.

Even writing God's name roots out the *vasanas*, and *smaran* helps to keep the mind flowing towards God.

I have seen how ego between lovers ruins their relationship. The one who says "sorry" first or takes the initiative is prudent. I have experienced moments when a simple "sorry" can solve many issues. But waiting to see who says sorry first leads to unwanted complications. Ego stands between "I" and happiness. Ego even edges God out.

Having been in contact with Sai for 21 years, I learnt why we need Him from the very beginning of our lives. I stress again that we need Sai not only after 60 but at 16 itself, even at 6.

It is Sai who inspired me to write this book for the youth, knowing well that there is no dearth of literature available on Him. The youth need a book that will link spirituality with human relationships; a book that is easy to understand; a volume that will not merely be another Sai book on the shelf.

Only if we bring spirituality into our present life can we hope to have a more fulfilling life and an even better future.

The myth that spirituality and normal life are different needs to be cleared. Spirituality is the same as our regular life. Spirituality makes us live our life as karma *yogis* according to the description by Lord Krishna in the chapters of the Gita.

The moment we talk about *gyan* or *agyan*, the youth lose interest. Once, in my confused state of mind, I approached a friend who was a renowned psychiatrist. He cleared my confusion with an example from the Gita. It was just one simple line in a two-minute conversation, but it made things crystal clear. He said life is not black and white, it is grey, that is, it has many nuances. Krishna uses these nuances to explain the riddles of life. If understood the way it is, Gita actually has the solutions to all our problems. *Bhagavad Gita – As It Is* by Swami Prabhupada – the founder of ISKCON (International Society for Krishna Consciousness) – is marvellous, simple, and a must-read for all. Thanks to it, I have no more doubts in my mind.

I chanced upon a celebrated photographer, who explained to me how he was full of positivity when he realized "why" he was born. Today, he is a happy soul and gives all credit to Sadguru's *kripa*. He realizes that what he actually wanted in life was to be happy and contented, not a part of the miserable rat race. Having come out of pain, he realized why he was here in this world. We exchanged a few thoughts on Sai.

Thus, spiritual discourse is not driven by time or place; it can happen anytime, anywhere, when *Sai Kripa* (Sai's divine grace) wills for it to happen. When we discuss *Sai leelas* with those who are interested, we feel extremely happy and derive immense contentment. The peace that envelops us then is the magic of the glorious *leelas* of the Almighty.

Sai asks me, time and again, why I fear when He is there. He tells me that every time I look at Him, He looks at me. He assures me that fear, though natural, is an inevitable hurdle in whatever we do. Whenever I am confused, Sai clears my doubts and communicates in such a manner that I can understand and act accordingly. This is a "connection" which all of us have to work upon and develop.

We study so much about different subjects. We try to gain an understanding. But, as humans, not surprisingly, we do fail some times. But then, we should be happy in the fact that, at least we tried. *Sai smaranam* (constantly remembering Sai) gives me intense *shakti* (positive energy). So much so that I feel I am a small Shirdi within my own self. Sai also said that one who sees Him only in Shirdi sees Him nowhere. Shirdi was a small village in the State of Maharashtra, India. It is now a town flocked by devotees from remote corners of the world. Sai had predicted this in *Sai Satcharitra,* that one day this village would feature on the global map and will be visited by innumerable devotees every day.

The more we take His name, the more we are able to discard the impurities which drive us towards the path of no return. The name itself has the power to heal and purify.

God is everywhere. He is omnipresent and omnipotent; the formless *Nirankar Swaroop*. When we say He is formless, it does not mean that He has no form. It implies that He has the ability to take on any and every form, which is beyond the human mind to understand or comprehend.

While we all try to understand, at times it may seem that we have failed. But, with our tiny steps towards the goal of our life and with the obedience to our Guru's teachings, we will continue moving ahead, slowly and steadily. Haste can cause difficulties in our progress.

Sai is the biggest blessing for me. His merciful presence is always there—I can feel Him; I breathe His name. He is everywhere—around you, within you, without you. Just knock at His door. He is waiting to let you in. If you can't knock, He will knock, but when He does, fulfil your karma of opening the door to let Him in. Without karma, what can He do? Karma is the basis of life and beyond. Please act. It is said that God may forgive you but your karma won't.

I have tried to cover some of my personal experiences in this book. I, through my own limited abilities, have tried to bring Sai to your doorstep. It is up to you to reach out and grab Sai's eternal grace, make your life beautiful and meaningful, and return to the abode of God, from where we all originated.

Given the limited span of life, do we have the time to argue or debate? Are mere 70 or 80 years of this limited life enough? Let us just not waste time arguing or debating. Actions speak louder than words. When personal experiences of Sai take place, we will not need any books of this type.

Sai will create, through His grace, a book out of your own life, which you will love. Subsequently, you will realize and appreciate how beautiful life becomes when His *leelas* are sung and shared. Sai explains in the *Sai Satcharitra* that when His *leelas* are talked about, *agyan* (ignorance) vanishes from our minds, and others are also benefitted. It is a simple plan to be practised. What is the benefit of going to a disco or pub, and dancing alone? Similarly, enjoy *leelas* with others and experience the resulting bliss. Sai never encouraged renouncement of worldly goods and escaping to a forest or a mountain. He said, "Be where you are, who you are, and I shall lift you, be with you, and take you to the path of renunciation in a way that things don't use you, but you use things."

When you understand and accept that there is, in fact, no need for a rat race, you will realize that each one of us is meant to be a winner—win Sai, win Him, and then you shall experience the reward of bliss. When you lose yourself completely to Sai, then shall you win the race. You will then want more and more of Him. Your thirst for Sadguru's *kripa* will never be quenched as you will always desire more and more. This desire is actually called "desirelessness", of which there is a frequent mention in the holy scriptures, preachings, and *satsangs*. However, beware of the many fake, self-proclaimed gurus, who promise you the ticket to a new and "transformed" life at the press of a button.

Why do you fear when I am here?

Chapter 3

Trust and Complete Surrender

We have to be willing to listen to the inner voice — the powerful voice of truth. But why don't we listen? While coins make noise, currency notes remain silent. Thus, at times, it is necessary to increase our value by becoming silent. In total silence, we are sure to hear the voice of Sai, who is actually residing deep within our heart. This is the concept of *Atma* (soul) and *Paramatma* (super soul) explained in the Bhagavad Gita. If we sit in a dark room and shut our eyes, then silence will speak to us, and speak the truth.

The thoughts in this book have been expressed with the intention of teaching others and also for my own self as well. Otherwise, ego will appear. If Sai wills it, He will do what He pleases and make me an instrument. Only in this humility can Sai, through this book, reach many, else it will just be an expression of my ego. The ego is a formidable enemy so we have to be aware of it always.

Dear readers, you will be surprised to know that for 21 years, no such thought arose within me, but suddenly one day Sai spoke from within, "Saurabh, don't leave the physical body without letting others know what you felt, experienced, and learnt." In the *Sai Satcharitra,* Sai told Hemadpant, the author of the book, that he will write on His behalf. Sai, in fact, modified the title "Hemadripant" (honorific title) to "Hemadpant" and told him that He made the alteration so that he does not nurse an ego that he wrote His *leelas*. Sai told him clearly that He Himself will be seated in his heart to direct him and make him an instrument. That is how Sai also inspired me. "I" started writing what came through Him as an experience and called it *Sai Saurabh,* where Saurabh was not me. "Saurabh" means fragrance. So, Sai turned my name into the fragrance of Sai—Sai Saurabh, who was re-born at 21 and wrote His *leelas*. I am convinced that my relationship with Sai has existed from previous births.

As long as we remain alert and don't let ego creep in, we are safe. If we fully surrender to Sai, then all will be well. However, complete surrender is very difficult. It is only through constant practice and *kripa* (ultimate loving grace) that we can achieve it.

It is the "I" which blinds us. I was religiously inclined from the beginning, but one day I realized that it was not enough. There was more to life than just religion. What was needed was spiritualism.

It is said that opportunities are like the sunrise; if you wait too long, they are gone. Therefore, wake up now itself. Realize why Sai, the Kaliyug Avatar, descended on this earth; why He is important and needed. Rise before it is too late, else you may be full of regrets.

Religion is often the first step of the ladder that leads to Him. But ascend the ladder slowly and steadily. Through experiences, the compassionate Lord awakens us and puts us on the right path through a true Sadguru.

May Sai hold our hands and take us all home—Home, Sweet Home. We need to return to the place from where we all originated. We need to experience the nectar of sweetness by going back to our original Home—the abode of the Lord; the place of no return.

It will be useful to mention the concept of love in the journey of self-realization and the example of Radha-Krishna is very relevant in this regard.

Radha is Krishna's Hladini Shakti. "Hladini" means internal energy of happiness and "Shakti" means positive energy. Therefore, Krishna is incomplete without His Radha, His loving energy. We can only experience real God through love, even though the form of love may be different.

Sai has helped me evolve; to realize that I revolve around Him. We should not expect the world to be fair, just because we are fair to the world. It is like telling the lion in front of us not to eat us because we are not eating him. The nature of the world is complex.

Having expectations is like being blind; then why be blind? If we cannot stop expecting in life, then we should stop expecting Sai's grace, too. Our expectations are far too low and less than what Sai wants to give or offer. When the devotee surrenders fully at the lotus feet of Sai, then all expectations cease and acceptance by Sai is obtained.

"All I want is someone who will be with me," I said to Sai, and he replied, "Saurabh, why are you playing with me? Just say you want me!" Make the Lord your companion and discuss your heart's inner feelings with Him in whatever mode you are comfortable. The Lord knows everything, it is true, but telling Him is essential to establish and grow a bond.

Sai, in the *Satcharitra,* says that "*Shraddha poorvak ek namaskar hi Mujhe paryapt hai*" (only one namaskar with full devotion is enough for Me).

Sai and Saurabh have a relationship which is beyond explanation. I am sure that every other devotee also feels so. Sai likes His devotees to have an independent relationship with Him. He never likes others to interfere. If the relations need explanations, then they are finite. How can then we be a part of something infinite? Surrender at the lotus feet of your Sadguru and you will realize why those feet are called lotus. It is because the lotus, despite blooming in the mud, is pure and offered for worship. It does not get dirty despite being in the mud. So, cling to the feet of your Sadguru and He will keep you away from the mud, which will be in the form of vices, and you will become like the lotus, fit to be offered at the feet of the divine Lord. Understand how the religious act of offering a lotus is linked with spirituality.

I love Sai not for what He is but because He loves me the way I am.

The relationship between Sai and His *bhaktas* or devotees is serene and divine. We often forget our real identity and limit ourselves to being finite. From a broader and truer perspective, we are in Him as He is in us. That is why we should not be asking Him what to do and when. Let us try to focus on how we can wholeheartedly surrender to Him and then there will be no need of any questions and answers. We humans limit ourselves through selfish and small wishes and become finite.

Eh mann tu jyot swaroop hai aapne mol pehchaan.
(O soul, you are like a flame of light, realize your real value.)

That is what Sai wants us to understand in our journey. Our *atma* is the pure form of *Nirakar* (Formless God). We are all pearls of the same string of *Parmatama,* we are all linked – *Vaasudev Kutumbakam* (the entire Universe is one family). In the same context, Sai mentions in the *Sai Satcharitra* the concept of *Rinanubandh* (indebtedness). He says, "*Rinanubandh ke kaaran hi hamara sansar mei janam hua hai.*" This means that because we are indebted to one another from our past lives, we are born in our present life. He further goes on to say that we, therefore, need to behave appropriately.

Ek noor se sab jag upja kaun bhalle kaun mande.
(From the One Light, the entire universe was born. So who is good, and who is bad?)

Gurur kripa hi kewalam shisyasa param mangalam.
(Guru's grace is the only thing for the welfare of a disciple.)

In the Ramcharitmanas, the devotion between Hanuman and Lord Ram is depicted very beautifully. I cannot be Hanuman, but I hope I can tear my heart and show to all how the smallest of things that Sai took care of are engraved in my heart. Where, then, is my fear of anything? Where is death? The Lord is more pleased with the worship of His devotee than His own self. That is the reason we will find more temples of Lord Hanuman worldwide than of Lord Rama.

It is so strange that today's youth light a cigarette in style, and even copy one another in the useless rat race, trying to show off and behave like their style icons. I met a girl, around 25 years old. Having my hands full, I requested her to light an incense stick for me. I was shocked to see her begin to light it from the wrong end. I had to tell her which end the *agarbatti* (incense stick) is to be lit! Where exactly are we heading? What teachings are we passing to our next generation? I am in not saying that religious practices are more important than being a good human being, but some basics are necessary.

Given the scenario today, nobody can be blamed. The parents themselves are lost. Earlier, a beautiful word, *sanskar* (values), existed. And *sanskars* were inherited by children in the family. But now? Children are exposed to the social media and the unlimited world of so-called knowledge, which has implications both in the practical as well as in the spiritual world. They need guidance on which choices to make. Once a choice is made, actions are performed and then karmic reactions are inevitable. Krishna has explained this concept of *chayan* (choice) in life very beautifully.

This is also the result of blindly following other cultures, thinking they are superior to us. All cultures have positives and negatives. Our Indian culture is scientific and logical. The others are only trying to understand spiritualism through us, while ironically, we are moving away from it.

"*Sab ka Malik ek*" (there is one Master), said Sai. So, where is the harm in choosing any suitable path to achieve self-realization? All that matters is that the path, which is correct for the destination, is the same for the entire humanity, irrespective of birth, caste, creed, and so on.

From the outside, we all try to smile and appear brave, but Sai knows that within our hearts, we are all searching for help. You just need to be yourself and Sai will mould Himself for you before guiding you.

What we seek is our true self. That is, in fact, the very reason for human birth. This birth is not to be wasted. Even the demi-gods are jealous, at times, of humans because only through the human form can God be actually reached. This is the difference between achieving *Swarg loka* (heaven) and *Vaikunth loka* (the real abode of God).

We have travelled through many lifetimes and lived with many different souls amid family, friends, and even foes. Some may have even tried to harm us emotionally, physically, or spiritually. However, we are all the same and belong to only one group, that is, souls. In the course of our journey, we come across and interact with people who are sent by God for our spiritual upliftment, but we may not realize this. Each person is a soul that tries to help the other move forward spiritually and reduce the karmic baggage.

We have all travelled together in different lifetimes and have shared various relationships with one another—father-mother, husband-wife, uncle-aunt, brother-sister, friends, neighbours, workers, and even so-called enemies. This is what was referred to as the concept of *rinanubandh* earlier.

Sometimes, the soul that loves us the most, might willingly take birth as an enemy or a tormentor in a lifetime, just to help us work out our karma. That is why, many times, the analysis of karmic reactions is beyond human intellect and comprehension. Total surrender to the Sadguru is the key. Make your life easier through surrender.

Thus, a person who we think hates us and we hate in return, might be our greatest well-wisher, spiritually. The person may be responsible for our becoming spiritual or compassionate. The very person who creates hell in our lives may bring us closer to spirituality. Very difficult to comprehend, isn't it? That is why Sai, in the *Satcharitra,* says that the journey of spirituality is like walking on the edge of a razor blade, and that is precisely why everyone cannot do it easily.

Sometimes, a soul is born just to comfort us and be there in times of need. So, who is our friend and who is our enemy? They are all part of the family of souls who want to help us and also seek our help in return. Only our outlook needs to be changed. Yes, it is difficult, but worth trying.

Who knows we may be harming the very soul who loves us the most spiritually, but we are unable to recognize it as the soul is wearing a different body in this particular lifetime.

Sometimes, an opportunity comes in the form of a disaster. Often, the only way to grow spiritually in life is by suffering pain, experiencing sorrow, and facing turmoil. That is when life seems strange. In our darkest phases, we need to realize and recognize the brightest light.

Hence, never judge abuse or hate. Never say nasty things about anyone. Sai, in the *Satcharitra,* states that the one who hurts a person's heart is actually giving pain to Him.

We must all understand that there is a huge difference between *nyaya* (justice) and *badla* (revenge). Justice is healthy, but revenge is very harmful. The difference between the two is very beautifully explained by Krishna to one of the most important characters of the Mahabharata, Draupadi.

After being humiliated by the Kauravas, Draupadi was burning in the fire of revenge. But this feeling was causing more harm to her than to the Kauravas who had committed the sin. That is when Lord Krishna, the Eternal Protector, told her that she needed to change her mind-set from revenge to justice.

Draupadi was devastated and deeply insulted when she was on the verge of being shamelessly disrobed in public. Seeing no help in sight, she surrendered to Krishna and was miraculously saved. Naturally, she wanted to take revenge, but was astonished when Krishna stopped her. Krishna explained that He was not asking her to forgive the Kauravas, but to simply convert her individual thirst for revenge to that of nyaya or justice. When you fight for justice, you are actually transforming your feeling of revenge into *dharma,* for then your actions are not for your own benefit but for the benefit of the society at large. The moment the intention of your action changes, the same karma changes into dharma.

Krishna made Draupadi realize that if she fights for justice, she will not only experience the eradication of pain, but will also help the society and become an eternal example for many *yugas* (eras). That is how Draupadi came to seek justice rather than revenge.

Revenge has become the motto of almost everyone in today's world, with most people on a short fuse. It can start from a road rage and lead to gang fights. It is difficult for today's youngsters resist revenge. However, revenge can only be justified if it becomes justice, and this is a very important difference.

As mentioned earlier, there are three types of karma. Sai alone can nullify our accounts of karma, of whatever so-called revenge that bothers us. We can leave it all to Him and ask Him to do whatever He wishes as per His will rather than consider it our revenge. If it is His game, then we are merely spectators. He is making things happen through us – things that He wants. But, it is very tough to leave everything to Him. Our immature supreme ego intervenes. But we should keep trying to attain Sai's guidance. He will also take care to transform our revenge into justice. If we endure pain to achieve the much larger purpose of humanity, the pain will not remain a pain but will transform into something better.

Another important thing Sai mentions beautifully in the *Satcharitra* is that *"Jaya maine jaisa bhaav taya taisa anubhav"* – according to our emotions, we have our experiences. This happens because our thoughts and feelings are read by Sai as He resides inside our heart. I have experienced this many times. For instance, I would be thinking that it had been a long time since I had *bhindi* (lady's finger), and when dinner is served, I would be pleasantly surprised to find *bhindi* on the plate. On the other hand, I am not really amazed as I know Sai reads my thoughts.

There is a very interesting and powerful *leela* of Sai in the *Sai Satcharitra,* where Sai reads the heart of a lizard and the devotees are astonished thereafter when they experience it in reality. Reading the 11th and 15th chapters of the *Satcharitra* daily, which mention such beautiful *leelas* of Sai, can transport us to a different plane. I have been reading those two chapters every single day for 16 years now and have had wonderful experiences. I have started living in those chapters now, so deep is my connection, so every day reading I feel was not needed.

Sai rules us from within. He knows our inner struggles and comes to our rescue by giving us strength. At times, He leaves us for a short while so that we try to catch hold of Him more firmly. If you leave a child, who is not very familiar with swimming, in the pool for even a second, the child will cling to you, not wanting to let go, ever. The same happens with Sai.

Whenever a negative thought crosses my mind or when I am disturbed, Sai miraculously appears to give me a message and takes away all my troubles. Such is His wonderful *leela*. The more we share them, the more we grow towards Him.

Sometimes I wonder how my life would have been without Sai—miserable, confused, depressed, directionless, and full of anxiety. Just today, I read in the newspaper that anxiety disorder may even lead to cancer. The very thought that Sai is there gives me the courage and peace, firm in the knowledge that I have nothing to fear. Yes, nothing to be afraid of at all. I am happy at the realization that I was so lucky to have found Sai in my youth. I cannot imagine what I would have missed had I discovered him later. My life would have been full of regrets for having missed the nectar of His blessings.

It has also become a fashion with the youth of today to proclaim themselves as atheists. Where is our youth heading to? Just as those who do not speak English fluently are often considered down-market, the youth today consider spirituality to be an up-market trend only if it is engaged in after 60.

The concept of Sai is very simple and practical as it is very relevant in the modern era. Sai encourages us to place total trust at the lotus feet of Sadguru, and Sai Himself will take the responsibility of all our burdens.

The problem is that we are not ready to trust Sai. Let us take a hypothetical example which will be very easy for everyone to understand. Suppose we are travelling in a train with heavy luggage. Once we have boarded, the luggage can either be carried on our head or be kept on the floor of the train. In either case, it is the train that carries the weight of the luggage, irrespective of whether it is kept on our head (putting us to discomfort), or placed on the floor of the train (while we enjoy the ride in a relaxed manner). If we do not trust the floor of the train, we will obviously prefer to carry the heavy baggage on our head.

You have to trust Sai, your Sadguru. Transfer the burden of life to His feet and enjoy the journey of life. He is here to take our burden. These are not burdens for Him. Of the famous 11 assurances given by Sai to His devotees, one is that all should cast their burdens on Him, and He shall bear them willingly.

By transferring our load to Sai, we are not escaping our karmas. It is impossible to evade karmas. By this, we are only becoming egoless and placing our complete trust in the fact that Sai is there to take care of everything. Sai is waiting to happily receive our load. That is the philosophy of *Sanchit, Prarabdh, and Karmana,* which is also highlighted in different ways in the *Sai Satcharitra, Bhagavad Gita,* and also *Srimad Bhagavatam.*

The entire Bhagavad Gita is based on questions and answers, but there is something hidden in this. The intention of the seeker (of the answers) is of paramount importance.

When in anger, I specifically think of Sai, and the moment I do so, He gets to know that I am desperately trying to seek His help and guidance. And in no time, He guides me, because I choose to give my burden to Him—a burden which He chooses to carry. The karma I perform then saves me from many negative effects; it ends up as a mature karma. Read each and every word of this book very carefully and the meanings will slowly be revealed through *Sai Kripa*.

This is very difficult, at times, to implement, but through constant trial and His grace, it can be done easily. When in anger, we need to remain calm and leave everything to Him. At times, even if we do become a little aggressive, He saves us by handling the situation suitably. Sai teaches us anger management beautifully.

He who trusts Me entirely and does not think of anything else is sure to attain self-realization.

Chapter 4

Shraddha and Saburi

Baba is omnipresent. At times, my mind is troubled by many burdens. But once I transfer them to Baba, I am at peace. He sends His message through others or sometimes He Himself appears to help through difficult situations. He loves those who talk about Him and spread His *leelas* far and wide. Who knows, by sharing His *leelas* some simple soul may get what he or she has been looking for.

Surdas, the eminent poet and devotee of Krishna, in spite of being blind, writes beautifully:

Charan kamal bandu hrirai,
Jaakee krpa pangu giri langhe,
Andhe ko sab kachhu darasaee,
Bahro sune mook puni bole,
Rank chale sir chatra dharai,

Surdas swami karunamay,
Bar bar bandu tihi pai.

For the one who is blessed by Srihari, impossible becomes possible, the crippled and lamed can cross the mountain, the blind gets to see everything, the deaf seem to hear, the dumb seem to speak, and the poor become royal. Surdas asks, who will be that unfortunate person who does not worship the feet of the Lord (Krishna)?

I firmly believe that where there is a will, Sai is the way. We should try to unlearn the useless things we have learnt and start afresh with no biases and prejudices. Let Sai guide us all and hold our hands through all our journeys.

A famous Sufi saint said:

Qyamat ke roz farishto ne jab manga ussae zindagi ka hisab,
Khuda khud muskura ke bola,
Jane do, Sadguru sei Mohobat kee hai isne.

(On the day of judgement, the angels asked the person for the account of his karmas. Then God smiled and said let him go, as he loved his Sadguru.)

This signifies the importance of the Sadguru in our life.

I like to define Sai as a faith or belief. Why? Because, in this logical world, the youngsters will not accept Sai till they are given a logic. They may even think Sai's role is merely to fulfil wishes. If He can't do so, what's the use of His existence, they argue. So, I re-iterate strongly that Sai is a faith. I, a modern-day educated man, have interacted with Sai for years, and through my own experience I am convinced of Sai's divinity. Mathematics fails at infinity. Sai is infinite and the finite human mind cannot grasp Sai. The entire process of getting to know Sai involves a slow and steady march towards full surrender, that is, *Shraddha* and *Saburi*—the most beautiful words taught by Shirdi Sai Baba. *Shraddha* refers to total respect and trust through love and *Saburi* refers to patience, with happiness.

This was the *dakshina* (payment or donation) Sai used to demand from His devotees. There is difference between *daan* and *dakshina. Daan* is charity with no ego and no expectation in return and *Dakshina* is the *Guru Dakshina* offered to the Sadguru as a token of gratitude and token of thanksgiving. Sai used to ask for a *dakshina* of two paise from His devotees. He used to reside in a dilapidated mosque called *Dwarka-Mayee* and said that one has to be free from the debt of *Dwarka-Mayee* (the mother and the door to the Supreme Lord).

I recall meeting a person in Shirdi who was 95 years old. I went to his hut, where he showed me a picture of Sai and him when he was eight. He used to play marbles with Sai. He even showed me the *Ganapati Murti* (idol of Lord Ganesha) which Sai had gifted to His ardent devotee, Shama (father of this 95 year old man). So, for those who want proof that Sai did come to this earth in physical form, this is a good proof.

Before Sai left His body and went back to His eternal abode, He performed some splendid *leelas* for the welfare of His devotees and others. He left His mortal coil on Vijaydashmi day, on October 15th, 1918 (Dussehra), Tuesday, at 2.30 pm.

I would like to repeat that in the *Sai Satcharitra,* Sai Himself says – I give people what they want, so that they can start wanting what "I" want to give.

People want something from God all the time. Such people are called *arthartis*. But God accepts all. He says, "You are dear to Me as long as you take My name." The faith builds, slowly. It often starts as some kind of a barter system.

Money is important in life for a *grahasth* (householder) as he has to meet all family responsibilities. In my career of nearly 20 years, I have come across people who pretend to be good and make false promises merely to achieve their own purpose. They think they are very smart. Sometimes, I get perturbed by such incidents. Money is, of course, your right, but it must be obtained fairly in exchange for services. But these are all worldly actions. At times, one has to fight till a point, then apply brakes, and leave people to handle their own karmas. That is the law of this world. Sai specifies in the *Satcharitra* that timely payment for *Parishram* (hard work) is a must. This is another practical teaching of Sai on how to do a profession or business.

Anger is difficult to manage. But the anger in me diminishes to a large extent when I see or think of the lovely picture of Sai. It may not be easy, but whenever we feel perturbed by the acts of someone else, we should offer our restlessness to Sai. He will protect us from negativity. Sai said, "Give all your negativities to Me" because Sai is like the sacrificial fire which purifies all impurities.

I think that as long as we offer all our deeds to God, we are safe. Let Him run His universe as He wants. It is His divine plan. We should make sure we act righteously according to Dharma. God will not put wrong people in our path Himself. We need to remember that He is always looking out for us. What is Dharma is a debatable question for some. Try surrendering yourself totally to Sai, and Dharma will reveal itself to you. Total surrender to Sai is the actual Dharma.

The journey of life is full of mysteries. Whether the Sadguru inspires our actions, or we decide to carry out the actions at our own discretion, is decided by the extent of our connection with the Sadguru. Only our heart can justify the intensity of this connection; it is something felt only by the soul.

I think it is necessary to dwell a little more upon the concept of Dharma—a word which is often heard and misunderstood, just like the word "Guru", which in today's world (Kaliyug), is used so flippantly. We often wonder who decides Dharma. It is a word, which the common person cannot understand. The true meaning of Dharma is understood when a person is spiritually connected. There may be no exact definition of Dharma.

When you are connected very closely to the Sadguru (Spiritual Master), He will reveal Dharma to you, to be understood and practised in all facets of life. When I say life, it includes worldly actions, as well as spiritual actions. In some cases, the Sadguru initiates the disciple and makes her or him ready for the spiritual journey. Then it is called "twice born". However, Sai did not do any formal practice of initiation of His devotees. To Sai, just remembering Him was initiation for the devotees. Faith is taking the first step even when we can't see the whole staircase.

All people should be drawn towards God. Sai may ask me whether I saved at least one life in my lifetime. Therefore, I can truly admit that I am being a little selfish by writing this book. One of my objectives is to be able to respond positively to Sai's question.

Thoughts come, but then we do not know if those thoughts are our own or guided by Sai. We act, and this is the catch, because actions are our own. It's very tricky. We all understand the compulsion to act. But if we surrender to Sai, He will guide us through.

When we accept that everything is happening due to Him, that God is everywhere and God is everything, that there is nothing but God, then everything goes well. This is the faith we have to develop.

When we perform actions out of selfishness, then it is our karma. If we leave everything to Him and say: What I am doing is what you are asking me to do, then the Sadguru comes into the picture as we are merely His instruments. To re-phrase Shakespeare, we are all actors acting according to the Director's wish in this play called life. Some people enter our life as blessings, while others arrive as lessons. Thus, in life, we never lose. Either we win or we learn (as long as we want to learn).

I always do *Sai smaranam* (remembrance) before going to sleep. His name and His feet give me peace, comfort, protection, and strength in every aspect of life. You can try it, too. Speak and discuss with Sai, Who resides within you. He is your anchor; establish an independent relationship with Him. He knows everything, yet tell Him everything for your own benefit and strengthen the eternal bond between you and Him.

We all need to enjoy every moment of life, especially because many times it is strenuous and excessively demanding. We are human and need to spend time with our loved ones in the real sense, not only through the virtual world. We should also take time out for what brings a smile on our faces. While the ultimate reality of our life is that we shall, whether we like or not, leave this body, we should live life in a balanced manner. Though Sai is with us in every karma, we should enjoy our karmas with Him and taste the nectar of *Sai Kripa* in all the actions we perform.

We should re-analyze what we are doing in life, and correct ourselves and our actions if we get caught in the rat race.

I sleep just as a baby sleeps, clinging to its mother. I sleep thinking I am actually in Shirdi in front of the Sai

Samadhi (His eternal tomb), clinging and encircling His feet, saying Baba *meri raksha karna* (protect me) and at times *mere avgun harna* (remove my vices). Then I talk to Sai and He takes me slowly into a trance. My negativities subside and I get the strength, peace, and courage to handle this unfair and harsh world.

In our life, with His blessings, we are able to stay detached and follow the righteous path. A wise person has said that even if you do not believe in God, you should create one for your own self to help you sail through this life.

I never expect anything from you other than shraddha (faith) and saburi (patience).

Chapter 5

Rinanubandh

We are all human beings with a mix of many different emotions. The degree and the nature of the emotions vary from individual to individual. My psychiatrist and psycho-therapist friend always said that any emotion in a limited amount is acceptable and normal. It becomes a disorder when the emotion overpowers you. Then, the emotion starts controlling you. That is the reason why Sai asks us to make Him the centre of all our thoughts and actions, so that He can absorb them. If we make Sai the centre of our thoughts and actions, we shall be driven by Sai, and the *aham* or ego of the *karta* or doer shall cease to exist.

I have witnessed Sai's guidance all through. I recall, years ago, when one night, I felt Sai so close to me, and with so much intensity that I had to request Baba to go away. I couldn't handle His presence and divine energy. I cried and said, "Sai, I am shivering and can't take your energy any more. Please, please go away!" But the feeling was divine and I still get goose bumps whenever I recall that incident.

Always remember that the intention of our karma, and the karma itself, will be our best friend or our biggest foe. Those who misunderstand karma think that they can get away with anything. But actually, everything else will be gone, except for our karmas. Power, fame, money, relatives, nothing will remain. God says, I may forgive you, but your karma will not!

If we are unable to find the answers to certain issues, or explanations to certain incidents, we get irritated; we feel disturbed, helpless, and angry. This is a perfectly normal human reaction. But if we surrender to the Sadguru at such a time, He helps us since He is always there for us and that whatever He does and will continue to do is for the best. Ignoring our negative thoughts is an important task, before we learn to ignore the gossip of the world around. It is said that we should ignore the thoughts that bother us and let them fly away, else they will return with double intensity.

I think it is necessary for all of us, including youngsters, to understand the concept of family, as observed through the eyes of Sai and mentioned in the *Sai Satcharitra.* I am sure all Sadgurus teach the same lessons. Sai defines our relationships and contacts through the term *rinanubandh,* which means we are indebted to one another for many lives, and that is how we come in contact with one another. Sai taught, through practical examples, how *rinanubandh* should be worked out. Every incident in life is a result of a hidden cause, which is being worked upon by the Almighty. So remember, *rinanubandh* is working everywhere in a very subtle way.

Make Sai the centre of all your thoughts, emotions, and actions.

Chapter 6

Material Wealth and Sai

It appears that the entire world is running after money. But can we ever say that money is running after us? Maybe we can.

The concept of *Lakshmi Narayan* is interesting. *Lakshmi* (Goddess of Wealth) is pressing the feet of Narayan, or Lord Vishnu, who is sleeping on the thousand-headed serpent, the *Sheshanag,* floating on the milky ocean. In simple words, it means *Lakshmi,* the Goddess of Wealth, is serving *Narayan*. That is why it is said that if we seek *Narayan, Lakshmi* will follow. This is a very important concept.

Further, *Sheshanag* over the milky ocean also has a notable significance. Many a times we find ourselves being controlled by vices, but later we realize that we shouldn't have fallen slaves to those vices. This realization, on its own, is a stepping stone to spirituality. The serpent, in this form, signifies that vices turn into virtues and they transform as we serve and worship Vishnu. The troubles of life can cause us no harm if we are protected by Vishnu, the Preserver. Milk is pure and it nourishes the body and soul, and so does the milky ocean. Sai, in the *Satcharitra,* clearly promises that there will be no dearth of anything in His devotees' lives. He acts as a complete protector and preserver. We should all read the *Sai Satcharitra,* which is a scripture like the Bhagavad Gita and the Ramcharitmanas. Read, understand, and then follow.

All that is happening is God's leela.

Chapter 7

Our Relationship with God

If someone hurts us, does it mean they were meant to hurt us? Or is it that we are paying for our karmas? Or is it a new karma which is unfolding? How do we react to people who are mean, jealous, and disrespectful? These are questions that plague our mind. They confuse and trouble us.

The point to understand is that the karma we perform is in our hands, but the karmas of others are not in our hands. It is *rinanubandh* that someone comes in contact with us. So, let us not show disrespect to others. However, if the other person is not behaving in proper manner, it is because she or he doesn't understand *rinanubandh*. From our perspective, we encounter a person or an incident takes place because the Almighty wants it to happen in that manner, for our own good. However, because the capacity of our mind is limited, this is often beyond our comprehension. That's why we call many incidents as *Sai leela. Leelas* (divine games or pastimes) can never be understood completely. All *Sai leela* aims is a complete surrender to the Sadguru—slowly, steadily, without haste.

The *Raas* of Krishna with Radha and the *gopis* (milkmaids of Vrindavan) is sometimes misunderstood. In brief, Krishna is the Supreme Soul, Radha is the love energy, and the *gopis* are the souls. The *Raas* is the union of the soul with the Supreme Soul of love. It is not a physical act but a representation.

Some situations are the result of our karmas, but even in these situations our Sadguru protects us. Our Sai comes to our rescue the moment we surrender our mind, body, and soul. He takes over from that point fully and it truly brings us closer to Him. As mentioned in the *Satcharitra,* sometimes our mother, Sai, gives us bitter medicine for our own good.

Sai is the *Kripa* manifestation of God. Whenever we think of Baba, He miraculously appears in front of us in some form or the other and blesses us or reminds us that He is always around. Even when bad thoughts enter our mind, He appears and helps us control them. Baba protects us if we serve and love Him with all our heart. *Shraddha* and *Saburi* always, is what Sai said.

Souls, who are directly connected with Sai, are blessed. People have no time for God in this day and age; they are simply running around. We should not make an excuse of being busy and having no time to connect with Sai. In times of need, no one will come to our rescue except our Sadguru.

In the Bhagavad Gita, Krishna said if we treat God like a friend, and we give ourselves up to Him completely, He will come to us for sure. That is what Arjuna did. He was completely dependent on Krishna, looking up to Him as a friend. And that is how Arjuna was able to achieve Krishna.

Krishna can be connected with us in the form of a friend, that is, in the *sakhya roop*. There are many other forms of connecting with Krishna. The choice can be made only by the devotee and Krishna himself. However, the conjugal form of love between a devotee and the Lord is the peak of feelings, and that's why Radha and Krishna are worshipped as one. Radha is the eternal consort of Krishna.

Be wherever you like, do whatever you choose, remember well that all what you do is known to Me.

Chapter 8

Sai Appears in Dreams

Sai can communicate with His devotees through dreams and also resolve the reactions of their karmic actions in dreams, so that the devotees do not have to suffer in reality. This uniqueness of Sai is also covered in the *Sai Satcharitra.*

I once had a dream that there was a *Sai bhajan* organized at my residence in the evening and I had invited many people to attend it. But, I dreamt, I lost the visiting card of the person in-charge of the *bhajan,* and there was no way I could contact her. As I panicked, beads of sweat appeared on my forehead. Even while writing about this dream, I can feel the same panic. What would have happened had the guests arrived? I even sent a person to the temple to ask for the bhajan team's number, but no one seemed to have it. Feeling helpless,

I went to my almirah and chanced upon a box, which I rarely opened. Inside it I found the card. I called the lady and she said she would come in the evening. I heaved a sigh of relief.

Though I am filled with anxiety every time I recall the dream, I thank Sai for taking away all the negativities from my karma in such a manner, and that too through a positive episode.

I would like to give another example of Sai saving me from karmic reactions through dreams. Several years ago, I dreamed that the buildings of the office where I work collapsed and everything and everyone was buried under the debris. The dream was so real that when I got up, I experienced sweat, pain, and restlessness as if the event had actually happened. The next day, I shared this dream with the owners of the buildings and we organized a *Sai Sandhya* (*Sai Bhajan*). I can only say that, ultimately, it was Sai who saved us.

I have experienced a number of other dreams where Sai has saved me. I have had innumerable dreams where the persons who have left their bodies have communicated with me and shared their messages, which I then passed on to the concerned individuals. "Thanks" is too small a word for His grace.

Hari Anant, Hari Katha Ananta!
(The Lord is eternal and so are His Leelas or pastimes.)

The *Brahm Mahurth* begins 3.30 am or so. It is a time when the sun slowly begins to show its presence through indirect ways, ultimately leading to sunrise. The calmness during such a time, for the meditator, enhances the force by which the thoughts are subdued. And thus, one achieves focus and single pointedness easily at this time.

Sai has always been there to guide me, whether to get me out of the most trying situations or to help me decide which path to take. Once a friend shared a small incident with me. It was a Thursday when she sat down to pray to Baba to help her find her father-in-law's briefcase, which had been stolen from under the car seat while his driver had stopped the car to fix a flat tyre.

And wonder of wonders – after about a week, some stranger called her husband and told him that a briefcase has been found with his card inside it. Her husband immediately sent someone to collect it. As always, Baba had answered her prayers. Not only was the briefcase intact, but so were the contents within!

Once a devotee asked his Sadguru why is it that when we usually take the name of God, we raise our hands up in the air?

The Sadguru replied that when a particular person is drowning in the deep waters, he always has his arms up in the air, so that someone can see and rescue him.

In the same way, we raise our arms to request God to help us and save us from drowning in this transient world.

For the one who is in Me, I am in him, said Sai.

Chapter 9

Lessons of Life from the Bhagavad Gita

The younger generation may not have interest in reading the Bhagavad Gita in detail. So I have given the important points in a capsule which they will understand easily. The following are the 18 lessons in the 18 Chapters we can learn from the Bhagavad Gita:

Chapter 1: Wrong thinking is the only problem in life.
Chapter 2: Right knowledge is the ultimate solution to all our problems.
Chapter 3: Selflessness is the only way to progress and prosper.
Chapter 4: Every act can be an act of prayer.
Chapter 5: Renounce the ego of individuality and rejoice in the bliss of infinity.
Chapter 6: Connect to the higher consciousness daily.
Chapter 7: Live what you learn.

Chapter 8: Never give up on yourself.
Chapter 9: Value your blessings.
Chapter 10: See divinity all around.
Chapter 11: Surrender to see the truth as it is.
Chapter 12: Absorb your mind and heart in the Supreme Lord.
Chapter 13: Detach from *Maya* and attach to the Divine.
Chapter 14: Live a lifestyle that matches your vision.
Chapter 15: Give priority to divinity.
Chapter 16: Being good is a reward in itself.
Chapter 17: Choosing the right over the pleasant is a sign of power.
Chapter 18: Let go; let's move towards union with God.

While I was trying to locate an earlier message about the above summary of the Gita, I saw that certain words were missing and I kept wondering how I could complete the message which I got as a forwarded text. To my surprise, within a few minutes, someone sent me a video on my mobile with exactly what I needed. How Sai Himself is making me an instrument to complete this book, is evident from His acts, whether minor or major. This is a very small example of how Sai intervenes for the benefit of the devotees.

One of my friends told me that he used to cry a lot standing alone in front of his Guruji because he was failing in interviews and his salary was stagnant. A few times, he even scolded his Sadguru. Before the end of one year, he actually got a 140 per cent hike. He used to feel that there was no progress for him anymore, till this happened and he started believing in His miracles. This incident meant a lot to him and showed his guru's grace in every sphere of life.

Never stop trying. Never avoid facing a situation headlong. Always try to get motivation from Sadguru alone.

Give up all your desires and meditate on the Lord. When the mind is focused, your goal will be achieved.

Chapter 10

Karma is Dharma

Karma karna hee dharam hai. Aur guru ko arpan karne mei kahe ki sharam?

Karma pradhaan vishv kari raakha, Jo jas karai tas phal chaakha.

Karma is the foundation on which the world is running. One will taste the fruits as per one's actions.

It is said:

Satsang is the start of life,
Sewa is the art of life,
Simran is the part of life,
Sadguru is the gift of life.

The more we realize that worldly actions performed for worldly happiness are like chasing a mirage, the more we will feel the need to introspect and question that if we are made to achieve bliss, then why suffer? This is the difficulty. Understanding that we are actually here to realize the self will take us forward on the path of bliss, that is, the path of self-realization. Thus, if at any point of time you are tired of the worldly miseries, awaken the thought that we are meant for bliss. Cling to your Sadguru, and He shall hold your hand in this eternal journey.

We must realize why we are here.

When people questioned the miseries and sufferings they had to endure even though all was in the hands of God, then Sai replied that at the time of *Srishti* (creation), the one thing that was given to humans was *ichcha* (desire). Instead of appreciating and admiring God's creation, people began to get involved more in *vasana* (vices). As a result, they were trapped in *Maya* (illusion) because of their own karmas. They deviated from their ultimate human aim, which was to reach God, and hence, the never-ending sufferings of life and death.

With the passage of time, as *adharma* increased, manifestations in the form of Sadgurus came to save humanity from suffering by directing them towards the goal of self-realization in order to realize God. But efforts have to be made by us, through *bhakti* and *gyan*, to realize that we, the Sadguru, and God are not different but all the same.

Please be ready to surrender completely and wholeheartedly to the Sadguru to reach God and see how life changes for the better, as peace prevails, love exists, and happiness grows, while we perform all our duties.

Even the fear of death vanishes. Remember, a Sadguru is most important for the practise of spiritualism.

Thus, dear friends, wake up before it is too late, as you came alone to this world and will have to leave alone. All you need is to look towards Him, and He will look towards you.

"I will not allow my devotees to come to any harm. If a devotee is about to fall, I will stretch my hands and support him. I will not let him fall." This is what Sai said in the *Satcharitra*.

May Sadguru's *kripa* fill our life with the colours of permanent bliss – a state beyond any pain. May the love of God reside in our hearts always and may it sweeten every moment of our lives with its sheer ecstasy.

Sai spread His message through colours of love, trust, care, happiness, and humanity. God may have many colours through *mukti* avatars, yet "*Sabka Malik ek*", Sai used to clarify quite often. We are all, in fact, manifestations of the same Almighty in different forms.

Whenever I feel low or frustrated, I try to speak to Sai. What can be more useful than sharing your thoughts with your loved ones? Blessed are those who have someone with whom they can be their own real self – no pretence, no judgements, just what we are. The irony is that today's generation has loads of virtual friends but no real friends.

In this hi-tech world of technology, we forget that the human touch and contact is very essential; we cannot survive without it. We cannot live completely in a virtual world. It is not important how many contacts we have in our phone book, how many likes we receive on Facebook; it is important how many we can contact to interact and connect with in reality. It's important to have people with whom we can share what we feel, how we feel, and who we really are.

Our basic composition is the same as that of God. We are eternal parts of Him. But unfortunately, if we try to tell our children or youngsters that Sai exists, they will first ask, "Have you seen Him? Can we talk to Him? Can you prove His existence?" Devotion and belief in God is left to the poor, the people in need, misery, pain, or trouble.

It is fashionable to give a cheque as a donation to charity and feel good about having done something for the society and boast about it. I am not trying to say that donating to charity is wrong, because money is an essential part of any activity. This is a fact that can't be negated. What I am trying to express is that the motive for a donation should be to ultimately connect with the Sadguru.

Connection is a process and needs to be understood and experienced individually. In my case, it is my beloved Sai. The moment you are able to connect with Sai completely, through every thought and karma, the entire life becomes a spiritual celebration. That is what I think is needed in this world today. Just as wi-fi is the easiest way to connect to the internet, Sai is the easiest way to connect with God, who is *one*, no matter by what name you call him by. Sai and Ram and Allah are one. Sai used to say "Allah Malik" very often and Sai is more popularly known as Sai Ram. That answers our question.

The Lord will protect him who possesses faith and patience.

Chapter 11

Age of Devotion

I would like to strongly object to the thought that devotion is to be practised after retirement. That is a very common thought. The retirement age may be 58–60, but why should we wait to reach 60?

Often young people debate that we haven't seen God or Sai, so He is not there. There are many things which we can feel, but not see. For example, hunger. I have not seen hunger, but I know how it feels to be hungry. And all of us know that hunger exists.

Jangal me mor nacha, kisne dekha is a popular saying in India. It means that if I claim to have seen a peacock dancing in the jungle, nobody will believe me, unless they see it with their own eyes. What I have seen and the other person hasn't, is false for them; it does not exist for them. But I know that I am right because I have seen it or felt it. Unfortunately, I cannot prove it. This only affirms that seeing is not essential to prove existence. Feeling is also a convincing way to realize that something exists.

We need to convince our own selves and our youth that just like we don't wait for retirement to satisfy our hunger—we do it constantly throughout our lives—it is time to realize and accept the existence of God and the hunger to be one with Him.

Please wake up, and according to your comfort, create a bonding with God through the right spiritual master. Just as food, which is not clean or cooked properly, can make you suffer from food poisoning, bogus or fake gurus, who claim to solve all your problems, can lead you to disaster. Such crooks are innumerable.

The law of karma functions in a very mystical way and since I have personally felt Sai and His presence, I can only vouch for Sai. I am no one to comment on others without knowing them, nor am I interested in them because I know for sure that my Sai is true and that is more than enough for me. He was there yesterday, He is there today, and He will be there tomorrow. He will even be there when this mortal coil will turn to the ultimate truth of ashes.

Only the persons who can feel Sai know what it is like to be a part of Baba. Baba is an integral part of us. You can call Him by any name. It is all the same.

It is said that we, at times, try to copy others. But life gives a different question paper to each person, so how can we copy answers written by others? That is the biggest mistake we do.

As mentioned earlier, Sai wanted an independent relationship with each devotee. He has carved a different path for each of us according to our capabilities, though our destination is the same. We can fly different airlines to reach the same destination.

Even children born of the same parents have their own distinct destiny and karmic journey. No two are alike. Each one has his or her own karmas to perform. The goal is the same, but the journeys are different. Meaningless comparisons in the materialistic and spiritual life is wrong.

Friends, karma is very beautifully explained in the Bhagavad Gita. Somebody may ask, "Why should I suffer now for my actions in a previous life? Why so much delay?"

Please remember that different seeds fructify at different times. Grains harvest after two or three months. Some fruit seeds produce fruit after twenty years, while some seeds may take just a year. Every action that we perform is like sowing a seed. The seed will fructify and we cannot escape the result. Even if we do not like the fruit, we will be forced to eat it, whether it tastes bitter or has thorns.

To understand this further, let's probe deeper into the mechanism of karma, as is illustrated through an incident from the epic, Mahabharata which I read somewhere.

After the bloodshed from the war at Kurukshetra, Dhritarashtra asked Krishna, "I had a hundred sons and all of them were killed in the war. Why?"

Krishna replied, "Fifty lifetimes ago, you were a hunter. While hunting, you tried to shoot a male bird, but it flew away. In anger, you ruthlessly slaughtered the hundred baby birds that were there in the nest. The father of the birds had to watch in helpless agony. Because you caused that father-bird the pain of seeing the death of his hundred sons, you too had to bear the pain of your hundred sons' death.

Dhritarashtra said, "Ok, but why did I have to wait for fifty lifetimes?"

Krishna answered, "You were accumulating *punya* (pious credits) over the last fifty lifetimes. To get a hundred sons requires a lot of *punya*. Then you got the reaction for the *paapa* (sin) that you committed fifty lifetimes ago." This is an example of the subtle ways in which karma works.

Krishna says in the Bhagavad Gita, "*Gahana karmano gatih*", that is, the way in which action and reaction work is very complex. God knows best—when to give the result for which action and in what condition. Therefore, as mentioned earlier some reactions may come in this lifetime, some in the next, and some at a distant or future lifetime.

There is a saying, "The mills of God grind slow, but they grind exceedingly fine." Every single action will be accounted for, sooner or later.

The *Srimad Bhagavatam* gives the following example: If we have a cowshed with a thousand calves and if we leave a mother cow there, she will easily find out which one is her calf from amongst those thousands. She has this mystical ability to find her offspring.

Similarly, our karma will find us among the millions of people on this planet. There may be thousands of people walking on the road but only one of them meets with an accident. It is not by chance, it's simply karma at work.

Thus, the law of karma works exceedingly efficiently. It may be slow to act, but no one can escape it. I would like to repeat that God may forgive, but our karma won't.

The Lord gives us good brains to use in this journey called life. He gives us the heart to feel love and spirituality. We are living in a world of hypocrisy and duplicity. Why are we trying to eulogize the dead and ignore the living? The chameleons in us with changing colours are superseding our own colour of peace and humanity.

The only way is to achieve ultimate salvation or *mukti* at the lotus feet of the Sadguru, else we shall be trapped in the vicious circle of *jeevan* and *mrityu* (life and death). We will waste this precious *manushya janam* (human life) if we do not hold the hands of our Sadguru and surrender at His divine feet.

Bus yehi bhool mein har baar kartaa raha,
Dhool chehre pe thi aur aina saaf karta raha.

(Through life, I kept making this mistake again and again. I kept wiping the mirror, while the dust was actually on my face.)

I think, this is why we are going wrong in today's world. This is why we are lost in the jungle of worldly and selfish desires. We have to choose the correct path, the right path to reach salvation. Sai blesses us all with the right choices in life. We have to forget selfishness.

While watching the serial *Siya ke Ram* on Star Plus channel, I observed how well Siya and Ram understand each other's thoughts and feelings. They know how to surrender themselves in love for each other. Even though in two different bodies, they are one soul. I hope this love becomes the basis of existence for all human beings. Only then will hatred and negativity in relationships be removed. I salute our rich culture and hope not only people experiencing a mid-life crisis, but even the youth understand this great concept. Radha and Krishna are the epitome of love, although this love and terms, such as *Raas Leela* are sometimes misunderstood and frivolously used as I have briefly touched upon earlier.

It is very tough for the youth of today to understand and accept this concept as they have their own unique queries. They think that these are all just stories and it is tough to make them understand their actual lessons. They think they are being realistic, but actually they are not. They behave as though they know everything and think that the elderly, especially their parents, are old-fashioned and lack knowledge.

Stories are eternal. They have a message waiting to be understood. When people realize this, they get enlightenment. Nobody can teach as well as time. *Samay* (Time) is very powerful. When you are keen and ready, God will automatically plan to open gates of knowledge for you and take away your *agyaan* (ignorance) to show you the light of the real truth—"Everything is God; everywhere is God, nothing but God" in me, in you, we all are one.

The human body is composed of five elements—earth, water, fire, air, and ether—and shall finally become ash or dust. The *atma* (soul) is our real self. In fact, *Srimad Bhagavatam* mentions the size of the soul. Take a strand of your hair, divide the tip into ten thousand parts. That one part is the size of the soul.

There are innumerable stories and facts where we see that the Lord has broken his own promise in order to save His devotees. The Lord is also more happy when the *leelas* or stories of His devotees are sung in comparison to His own *leelas*. The vow taken by Krishna in the epic Mahabharata, that He shall not raise any weapon during the war is broken when He tries to kill the senior most member of the Kuru dynasty, Bhishma Pitamah, in the battlefield, to save Arjuna. Another example of devotion, I would like to repeat, is that throughout India and the world, we see that the temples of Lord Hanuman surpass those of Lord Rama. The *Hanuman Chalisa*, written by the famous Saint Tulsidas, is sung or chanted in every Indian household. The concept of mirror and dust is very clearly defined in the first verse. The first few lines of the Hanuman Chalisa are as follows:

Shri Guru charan saroja raj nija manu mukuru sudhaari.
(With the dust of the lotus feet of my Lord, I clean the mirror of my heart every day to see reality.)

Jug sahastra jojanpar bhanu leelyo tahi madhur phal janu.
(Hanumanji gulped the Sun, at an average distance of about ninety three million miles, considering it to be a sweet fruit.)

The distance between the Sun and the Earth was calculated in our scriptures long before scientists calculated it, such is the greatness of our scriptures, which are being neglected by the youth of today.

Youngsters may feel that these are just poems in praise of the Supreme Lord. However, if you go into detail, you will realize that each verse has a deeper meaning, apart from the literal translation. It is all very scientific as well.

There is a story of a thirsty crow, which we often tell our children. The crow was unable to reach the water at the bottom of a pot. However, he smartly puts pebbles to raise the level of the water in the pot to enable it to drink it. Children study science and ask why the level of the sea does not rise even we throw many stones and pebbles in it. Stones and pebbles do make the sea rise.

We simply don't have the eyes to see the phenomenon. As mentioned before, questioning is not wrong, but the motive behind the questioning is what matters.

Often, knowingly or unknowingly, we leave things to God. He is the one who gave us life and will also give us all the awareness to connect to Him. As parents and well-wishers, we can only guide our children, but we should know when and what kind of guidance is required. When the time is right, children should be prepared for their spiritual awakening. They need to be made ready. We need to have faith in Baba's "wake up" call, and the situation will change for the better. Krishna spoke about how destiny is nothing but the accumulated results of karma.

The action of Bharat in the Ramayana of dragging his own mother, Kaikeyi, out of Ayodhya when she banished his favourite brother, Ram, into exile for 14 years, signifies how our karma will eventually transform into reality, irrespective of our relationships. The entire concept of spirituality revolves around this eternal principle of actions and reactions, sooner or later. This entire book revolves around the concept of karma and Sadguru Sai.

When we believe in this, many of our questions, such as "Why me?" get answered. In happiness, we never raise this question, but in distress we immediately ask, "Why me?"

The key lies in filling yourself with gratitude. Questions will cease once you reach a point where you won't require any answers. Such is the difference between total faith and blind faith. It is said, "*Shukrana Prabhu ka aur sada muskurana*", that is, we should always thank the Lord and be happy.

Remember that our thoughts become our karma and, eventually, they become our destiny. So what we create is what we get. What goes round, comes around. Our life is all about our choices. So, there should be no blame game.

The moment we start accepting that whatever is happening in our life is the result of our own actions, peace starts creeping in through this logic. People are nothing but the medium for our reactions.

Let us use our free will for actions to surrender to Sadguru. We should all keep trying. The moment we take responsibility of our deeds, we feel so much lighter. We get out of the blame game totally.

I can vouch that Sai really helps. I try taking His name with every breath. Even though proof is not needed for His presence, He makes it a point to let us know that He is there with His devotees. Every relationship, in some form or the other, is based on the real principle of give-and-take.

A devotee from Jaipur once told me that when he saw my message with Baba's picture, he started crying, because just before he had woken up that morning, he had seen exactly the same image in his dream. Imagine, what he must have felt! We should stop calling such occurrences coincidences. These are, in fact, communications between the devotee and his Sai.

I recall the day when an elderly woman, who was a cancer patient, was sitting outside my residence on the pavement, with her daughter. She had come and got an MRI done. The lady was breathless. I believe it was Sai who made me go outside at that moment and notice her, because I usually don't go out like that. When I saw her, Sai inspired me to send my driver to drop her home. I knew it was *Sai leela* and thanked Him profusely for making me realize that some people in this world don't even have the basic resources, while we, on the other hand, become thankless and take things and people for granted.

The world is becoming rather thankless to God. We take God for granted. We all need to have Sai on our side, from our early days in life itself. Who has seen that old age, which may not even come? We should not wait to become old to spend time with and for God.

We should stop expecting *meva* (dry fruits) out of *seva* (performing selfless deeds).

Karna, from the epic Mahabharata, did not wish to be called *Kunti Putra* (son of Kunti) because he believed that the karma of Radha, the lady who raised him as her own child, was far superior to that of Kunti, who had abandoned him after giving birth. Don't confuse this Radha with the Radha (Radhika) who was the beloved of Krishna. That is why Karna preferred to be known as *Radheya,* and not *Kaunteya.* This is thus, another example of karma playing a major role. A similar example is that of Lord Krishna, who is more famous as Yashoda Nandan (Son of mother Yashoda), who raised him and took care of him, while it was Devaki who actually gave birth to him.

Banns sab hote hai lekin bansuri banne ke liye ghav khana padta hai baans ko.

The *Bansuri* (flute) is light because it is hollow and has holes. It has nothing of its own. Krishna plays many beautiful tunes on it because the *bansuri* has surrendered to Krishna and is empty from within. It has no ego, no voices inside. Also, the *bansuri* has to endure the pain of the holes being drilled into it, only then is it able to produce music. Similarly, if a devotee doesn't become a *bansuri*, how will his life be made musical by Krishna? What a beautiful example! We often wish to play the flute in our own unlearned capacities, and the result is noise.

From clutter, find simplicity. From discord, find harmony. In the middle of difficulty, lies opportunity. Nothing is good or bad, it is our thinking that makes it so. You must look at everything with a correct attitude and find goodness and delight everywhere. Positive thoughts and the feel-good factor will bring you joy and happiness.

Tulsidas, in the Ramcharitmanas, says, "*Jaki* rahi *bhavna* jaisi *prabhu murat dekhi tin* jaisi", that is, God will take the form in which your heart intensely desires. Sai said the same thing in the *Satcharitra*, "*Jaisa bhaav raha jis mann ka waisa roop hua mere mann ka"*. In the *Sai Satcharitra*, we find many examples of this, including the times when Lord Sai gave His devotees *darshans* in the form of Lord Ram, Vitthal, Krishna, and so on. Ramcharitmanas was written a long time ago by Sri Tulsidas. *Sai Satcharitra* was authored much later, not even 100 years ago, by Hemadpant, but the concept is the same. Do we need any further explanation?

Truth is unchangeable. It is always the same, in any era. It may come from different mouths, but irrespective of the religion, truth will remain constant.

That is why, God teaches us to be honest, and without any double-faces, so that we see Him everywhere, with our *shudh bhavna* (pure feelings). Then we become reflective mirrors of His goodness. We resonate His *swaroop* (infinite form), and reflect Him everywhere we go. We are in Him and He is in us. This may sound difficult, but we should simply keep trying to understand.

All times are good as long as we have the *drastic* (vision) and can realize that Sai has a purpose for all incidents that occur in our life.

Kaha karau vaikunth lai, kalpabruchh ki chhah,
Rahiman dhaak suhawano, jo gal pritam baah.
(According to Saint Rahim, there is no point in going to vaikuntha and sitting there under a wish-yielding tree. It is better to sit under an ordinary tree with someone who loves you.)

Another important couplet by Saint Kabir is:
Guru Gobind dou khade,
Kaake laagun paaye,
Balihari Guru apne,
Govind diyo milaye.
(Guru or teacher and Govind or God are both standing in front of me; whom should I bow down to, first? The Guru, because he is the one who introduced me to Govind or God.)

Sai helps all the time, but without trust we cannot realize this support. Children should fear parents, but not be scared of them. The difference between fear and scare needs to be understood.

For the readers to know, there exists a Sansthan (institution) in Shirdi called Shri Sai Baba Sansthan Trust (*www.shrisaibabasansthan.org*). It publishes *Sai Satcharitra*.

Let's all do something to spread the word of Sai the way Sai wished. Sai created the *Sai Satcharitra*. Let's understand the significance of the book, each word within its pages, especially Chapters 11 and 15, and feel close to Sai. These two chapters changed my life as I started reading them daily and in my personal, professional, and spiritual life, I have been really blessed by Baba. In brief, I would like to say that in my personal life, I have become a better and a strong human being, in my professional life, I have attained loads of success, and in my spiritual life, I am trying to realize my own self.

We need Sai Forever... at 6, 16 and 60!

Let's all get together and experience Sai's presence near us. People have been going to Sai. It is time to now let Sai come to us.

I would like to request each reader of this book to pray to Sai for me as well, so that I am devoid of any ego arising from the fact that I wrote this book or Sai chose me as the medium for this book.

As I always say, do your best and let Sai do the rest.

Sai Bless!

Do not worry. Whatever is destined to happen, will happen.